"I have never read anything like this.
It is unpredictable, weird, profound, witty, and intelligent.
I just love where this stuff takes me.
Truly original."

Benjamin Zephaniah

DOESN'T EXPECTING THE UNEXPECTED,
MAKE THE UNEXPECTED EXPECTED?

CONDIMENTS
&
ENTRAILS

JOHN DURAK

In all probability an unfinished mixture of
words, stories, and a few poems . . .

A special nod of appreciation without saying & saying it goes to:
Denis for keeping track of all my parallel selves. Siniša for being honestly
interested for such a strange project. And not least—Nataša & Ivana without
whose kind understanding nothing of this would ever come out of my
mind into the obscene reality we all inhabit. Dalibor for taking
some time off his vibrant lives to grace this book with his art. RazTomo for
being patient and understanding despite all the surrounding fuzzy logic delay.
And definitely last—everyone trying to stay in balance while
outbalancing all their opponents and being aware that those are
actually their alternative selves.

#johndurakwashere

Copyright © 2022 by John Durak

Edited by Marko Škobalj & Buzz Poole

Design & Art Direction by
Denis Kovač

Illustrations by
Dalibor Barić

Published by
Sandorf Passage
South Portland, Maine, United States
imprint of
Sandorf
Severinska 30, Zagreb, Croatia
sandorfpassage.org

Printed by Stega tisak, Zagreb

Sandorf Passage books are available to the
trade through Independent Publishers Group:
ipgbook.com / (800) 888-4741.

Library of Congress Control Number:
2022930386

ISBN: 978-9-53351-371-3

To the Unfortunate Wife

I am neither my writing
nor thinking; nor fucking;
but am in between

Sitting while words
−playful in Art revel;
a person that is me−awaits

Full moon rising at my doorstep
above & beyond = nothing;
shouting & kneeling; deeper, deeper feeling
you, all–listen! we are coming
it's a full moon rising

Shipwrecked on a rock steady burden
of a question—
why does a bug crash into a windshield?
is it to save the sleepy driver
is it to uncover society's angst
through self sacrifice or simply to make
that squishy sordid sound

My name is my own
no other has the same
where would Zeus be
if called Avalanche;
surely not at the top
Oh, such pity! a blunder happened,
the way I had to remember mine…
yours, I already forgot

Thin sluggish crust oozes over
screams/sirens
the strength of the abyss which/witch
finds hope in loosing the Mind; at the same time;
faith is a worm worn thin crawling across fear's Ave.
unhelped from the Heart

When I die; whenever
into that singularity I will dip strong;
yet fearful; your face clouding the country;
your smile–unconquered;
but when I die it will take
an unmoment to realize your presence behind;
never say a word: "just slip your arms around!"
I will shudder–overwhelmed;
Clearly the smell of life to come
…I died

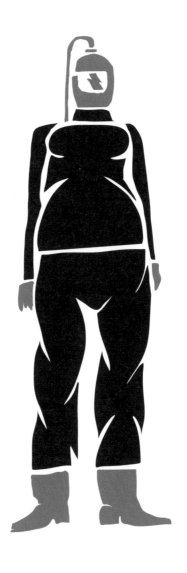

Met G.O.D. once minding my business while
handling poorly a drink in a pub;
he just returned from snowboarding in Vermont
& wasn't much of a stud
(natural truth or artistic lie)
he's a big fan of *Star Trek*
(now, isn't that prosaic)
naturally, he drank only tea and stood in his own time
(hard reason or blind faith)
tried to anger him cursing pitifully
and got only a raised eyebrow
our G.O.D. is a forgiving one
as he wanted to leave
I started to cry axing: "Will it hurt, God?"
on the way out, he replied:
"You cannot hurt god, only make it smile."
and went out while I stayed in & cried myself out

For hrs. I read Dokan saying these words aloud:
   "Had I not known that I was dead already,
    I would have mourned my loss of life."
& then I burst my skin with a needle so strongly
    I simply wasn't anymore

A ship on a mountain sails
to Heaven's glitzy
edge it transcends
a night escapes far away

Sitting in a field of cows
their shrieks—a constant
restless
it has been far too long
since I sat with I
skies imploding
mind exploding
possibility of becoming
MOO! MOO!—a constant
elementally charged
agenda: subject & object united
"reality"—a patchwork
feeling sweet Nothingness;
like Nowhere else
mu! mu!
complete

Like a stupid B-movie prop
a body is pulled under a wall
dead body in dead silence
should be for the dead

Herehere hereherehere.
hairhair hairhairhair!
harehare hareharehare?

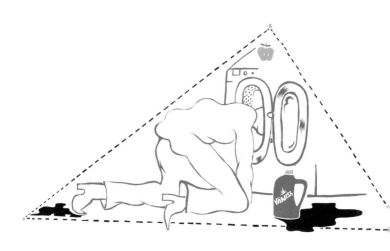

Yellow window within my reach;
a sky is falling over

Colorful offerings on a long round table
beddings empty, corridors peaceful
every bite readily fast upon as muted stomachs whisper
food: squidgy, sour, sweet—whatever!
while the ever fresh feast is served
she leans closer with sweet scent of mimosa
wafting from her jet hair
softly speaking to me
for them potential physical love coming nearer
but the two of us are making out
masticating
transfiguring

Just after a postponed resurrection
among the people;
tensed, as my father's succubus
penetrated her sweet surroundings,
bold and gold playthings
spawned acid plights undulating weakness
Would I not be a stylish divinity?
if not for my genetic impediment—
high mortality rate

Ass watching
womanizing stance
progressing fine tuned
Sound—off key
What?
road works' trembling frequency—
liquor that binds me whistles:
"Women are not hard headed
they are simply more consistent."
epiphany pif pif…
why does it sound so like a sound?
sound that my brain
pictures within my mind
like Snagglepuss I dash elsewhere for another sign

Shooting sperm over master's slippers
not realizing he forgot to lift the curtain
blind motion, Newton's laws, Copernicus
—bastards all!

Sudden drowning in another person's psyche
in between reason
notwithstanding scythe
physiological homeostasis
spirits balancing
white noise of a subspaced
pure thought basking in the reverse;
boulder of the universe rolling down,
up and inside out

In neon's bright
pit-a-pat—I shat;
dense soiled cavities
(children of stars self-made)
zenith's rebels
change of balance is how it is all achieved
black turd hole (not 3rd eye)
bestowed/branded on foreheads
sucking each person's shit,
using the other orifice to retort the same
but sure as your mama...
we never listen—never hear
never see—just talk
never participate—never anticipate

As a poison cup
opposed to a placebo;
turmoiled mind play of leaves;
unexplained influence music has on a soul;
everything is revealed and still;
most people want to be most other people
not sensing we are each other's mirrored neutrons
tantalizing magic creating magnum opus that is Godhead

Emotionless–staggering in waves of Motion;
being surfaced by lack of Distance
my heart stuttered
my soul defrocked of pearls
I am in NYC by a pond
needing a bond
badly

Thinking of a gentle friend;
on an island in a sea;
planting life to be;
but me;
alone in a sea;
sitting on an island that is me;
witnessing sharks biting their nails
in shallow waters;
afraid of what is to be

Two tornadoes making love
spilling cool into each other
over a parting fence of a sloped razor that
points to crevice filled with ammoniacal juices
two soft pillowcases filled with red pulp
ripe for saving
body of Helena I'll possess
with style
getting hard between your eyes

Have never seen so frightful a scene
as when approached by my face
surrounded with fast moving innards
of grey worm's strutting grace

First we ate
then strolled around
watching & exploring, buildings transfiguring;
pools of glistening glass;
playful yards all the way to the clouds
heaven was on a 45th fl. and yet, our fall;
our fall mercifully buffered before
hands sweating as we zoinked to the Hellish hall
and cooled our soul in an architectural sanctuary
On! We stepped! Ourselves no more;
lost in Nature's hideaway;
surrounded by mute mercenaries of Hi-Tech godlings
waiting for the climax of better times;
a moronic prophet disguised
as green viper alerted us
pointing out the Pulse—then we ate

Slurping last night's
revealed truths
my tongue dipped in dark beauty;
laziness leaning on a balcony of thought
easily grooved into forgetfulness
cascading over sexual deliverance;
Sun—a timeless loop of a cult long extinct
offering: stranger's godlike stare…
perky ass, too

(Wisconsin)
iris of a pupil
black & blue
of your eye
(Vin's cousin?)

Through rhythmic annihilation
(head bobbing here & there)
saw an apparition;
a black panther gently crouched on a rail
nostril's pulsating, never failing:
beauty wild, the depth of which
in rhyme in sleep
in my mind
I cannot reach

Subjectivity is the
resonance of objectivity
I know, for I have burst
soon, Mother Earth will follow.
we are both having THE flu
—wipe our noses if you dare
if not
leave us be

If only pitchers
were women's breasts
I'd be the most famous lover of all

Walking a dolly
not with capital D;
sheesh;
it is easily that lady's luck
& misery being towed down
the 5th that got chronicled here

Sauerkraut just next to the bacon.
why isn't than an egg nearest to the ham
or milk just beside corn flakes?
—before Meltdown
computer is aware
& will understand these patterned soul bytes finite
in light of a foul moon crashing
to her these were trivialities

Catching flame with the Eye
wind is strong, fire weak
mind—a constant flicking thing

Stepping over chrysanthemum opium fields
a museum scene developed before my peepers wide
patched of Reality fabric;
the question emerging with a tear–

if a butterfly's wing
could cause an airplane crash,
what can you expect of a cage crowded full
with the seething madness of these fluttering beasts?

Doubts piled enormous
somersaulted from divinity
into shattered psyche
into restaurant calm
relax!
left without an anchor
got stuck in the dead
center of my throat chakra
laughs all around
clockwork guinea pigs–whisper!
infinite key dial clicked
couldn't find full stop
in between thoughts as they streamed
from any each way
–only needed to talk & share

Vacuumarium of souls dancing
pulled by G-force
what music are they creating

G.U.T. feeling is sometimes hard to swallow;
anyways; still walking the Earth
collecting stares in my porcupine bag

If you ask me
this multiverse in DTS
this conceptual grinder we dare to call life;
is but a tennis shoe made to resemble
a shoe resembling a tennis shoe;
it is a fluke!

If I were to write a poem
most gentle:

1. I'd take a frostbite harvested morn' fresh
2. Betwixt 2 shards of a Soul—squeeze it so!
3. Take this contraption 2 the Spring of Youth & "Lo!
4. Your lips R meant 2 shout:
"Aye, strike me dead now, in beauty whole
here naked in nature's call."
5. Throw, then thy heart 2 the Love—unrelenting

upon returning home;
there on my bed would lie my body
with succulent grey streaks coming from my head
music swelling from walls lethargic &
wisped to a black hole
my essence microscopic
would crawl into a firefly's intestine
—fluorescence incarnate
gleaming over my son's cheeks
nearing the witching hour
of his shedding Ego

Loris eyes & poked entrails;
sweating fatherly Cyclops
maddening on a deserted cone
click–clack
wider perspective!
minding the wind that backtracks the page
just for me: gods bellowed–
"Come now, you cannot escape your limitations."

Morning dew
doo—whoopty—doo
trying to put nature into words
failing in all majesty
oh, happy me!
killing thirst, sounds & visuals
turning bravado into mind casket while
Miss Conception greets me with her bitchy ways

grabbing roots for help & passing out furiously

Grazing downers lazily
uppers too high to reach
a pocket in my skull needs a zipper
to stop the nonsensical attack of circumstances
that are simply too much to have for lunch

Imagine being a clash of stares
between two husks of human detritus
scared not yet dead
looking/getting more scared
former selves–forgotten
present reality: whiteness, dusk & pity

Starry night
off Kathmandu
trailing south
Kali satisfied
consciousness impregnated

Chirping monkeys.

seen dead
touched dead
eaten dead
smelled dead

cackling monkeys.

Hawk spirals through kites,
a building breaks not its soar
hawk is a soar

Golden flow to damp grey
sand–the obvious transcend

A cloud surpassing enormity of fluid
perpetually gaining on violent Sun with sporadic ricochet

crown
yet cruel
soggy arousal
clutching at pelvic
adamantium core

a crow
thumped
slushing
resonance
yogini realized

kraw—kraw

Rolled on a baby fresh morning
sphincter tense
a newcomer enters the vacuum
eternally pressured my smile reflects
dawning rays

shitrocked
indeed!

What an amazing riddle solving
crabs partake coming home
day & night
dark or light

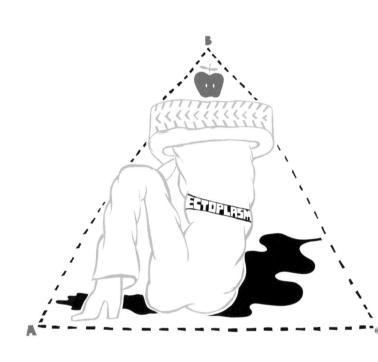

As it were
I went insane
as the snowflake
touched my brow
as it were
I am
forever
now

If I had no legs,
would I be purged enough to
freely touch your shrine?

Ideal boil
that you need
for an outburst of the idea
is the room temperature

what an afterthought?!

Paying the dead man's
electrical bills
illuminates me to say:
grave is not a free enterprise

Hair between a page.

a metaphor
skids over the ledge
like a true summer pledge

With one mighty swing
potentially
ulcerated
my person expected your carnal causality
stripped and basking in moon fire
waiting like a fat ugly spider
in a nylon web of the night

As for me
I could leave the world
with today in my eyes

When winter hits high
—quite naturally
I'm used on transforming heat
from her thigh

In her chest
does dwell 7 demons of Hell
each for a day of the week
making her vulnerable & divine
while I feel utterly sick with devotion

While reminiscing on a deck
—a thought occurs
with whose transforming might
I become;
a demon haunted planet
devouring full moons
into everlasting night

Titanically inclined and overly pressured
my toes exploded
into the unsuspecting world

—taken by surprise
it shuddered

The day has gone
in a bubbling realization
while the night

has come
with auspicious
nullification

Frozen cobwebs
of false emotions
stretch the narrative
until the rapture
descends its hand
innovative

Teeny tiny mousy Moe
first naively
lost his toe,
then came:
hair, tit & soul;
while dark winds did blow;
hear closely
—in winter his pains
that Roar

Another major crisis
(Have I a thing for goddesses):
on a crowded square
my soul brushed
a pearly skin of Isis

Thirsty fat & obsessive fly
drinks each dawning
an adhesive droplet from the eye
furiously debilitating–compulsive;
I, must again resume to cry

I proclaim most assured
that when pseudo pressured
my headgear lacks
the self...
confidence

Ego delivered western style
has to be handled
as a kind of robust
piece of intimate accessory

Unaided, in a tremendous
fire of a dream;
reluctant:
I resigned from the heavenly station

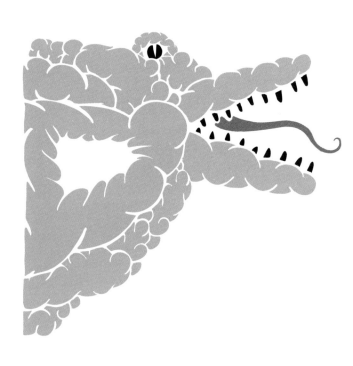

Cleaved post modernity
stripped to its romantic heart
resembled my pitiful intellect
in tensed equilibrium
hovering over the Arab market
—full of fruits, shouts & odors
in a dream of a dreaming river

Creation might be
an answer to me
—a problem to start with:
it is just a construct
believed into existence

Vivisection as a complete
absence of life
—respect devours
labor/enormity
in sheer presentability
of death—joy persists unconquered

Thank you Eye;
for the possibility
of a self less
conquering constant

Wore my robe: rubies & all
when dark blotched
eyes turned then
stared trying but
failing to steel
my delicious probe
fleeing through ironed
woods I moved in action
feeling stilled
my texture–universal
my light–everyone's to see

Feels like driving in mute silence
with thunder for a roof
never quite sure in the grand search
for never before seen marbles

nearing another bend

Bag of nerves entered a kidney clinic
looking for resolution
but ended up
inhaling acid solution
attaining free downpour of depression manic
what an illusion!
this reality shows parts
undefined by the whole

Wistful breeze round my neck
like a shawl
squeaky reassuring sound
made to resemble a ball
whose trajectory is off heaven's lights
tugging at my soul
as eyelids gently drowsily fall

Since I last saw you, I have lost;

sense of fun/humor/adventure/taste
some hair
enthusiasm for life
lots of hats
memory
conscience
27 mobile phones
2 motorbikes
my way
misc./other

Dark splendor in delight:
hook is deeply burrowing
a point where two curves meet
—extracting wine of gods
with silky entrails;
offered at your altar

Begging for peanuts
an insecure dwarf
in the searchlight of fear
while ego peaks
through fat woman's thighs

Shadow linked to my existence
forever bound in craving
the everlasting

Stalled away in van Gogh toilet
doing the inventory list pad consisting of:
1 concrete painting; 2 and a half bone sculptures;
6.5 pain-seeking nuns–
in the Mind run
I am the marathon Man

To what cause
this life of yours
affects thy?
asked the moralist;
scornful
—then whispered the artist;
calm:
precious little
darling
but
I love you so

John Durak is a graphomaniac
of whom nothing is known.

Sandorf Passage publishes work that creates a prismatic perspective on what it means to live in a globalized world. It is a home to writing inspired by both conflict zones and the dangers of complacency. All Sandorf Passage titles share in common how the biggest and most important ideas are best explored in the most personal and intimate of spaces.